DATE DUE

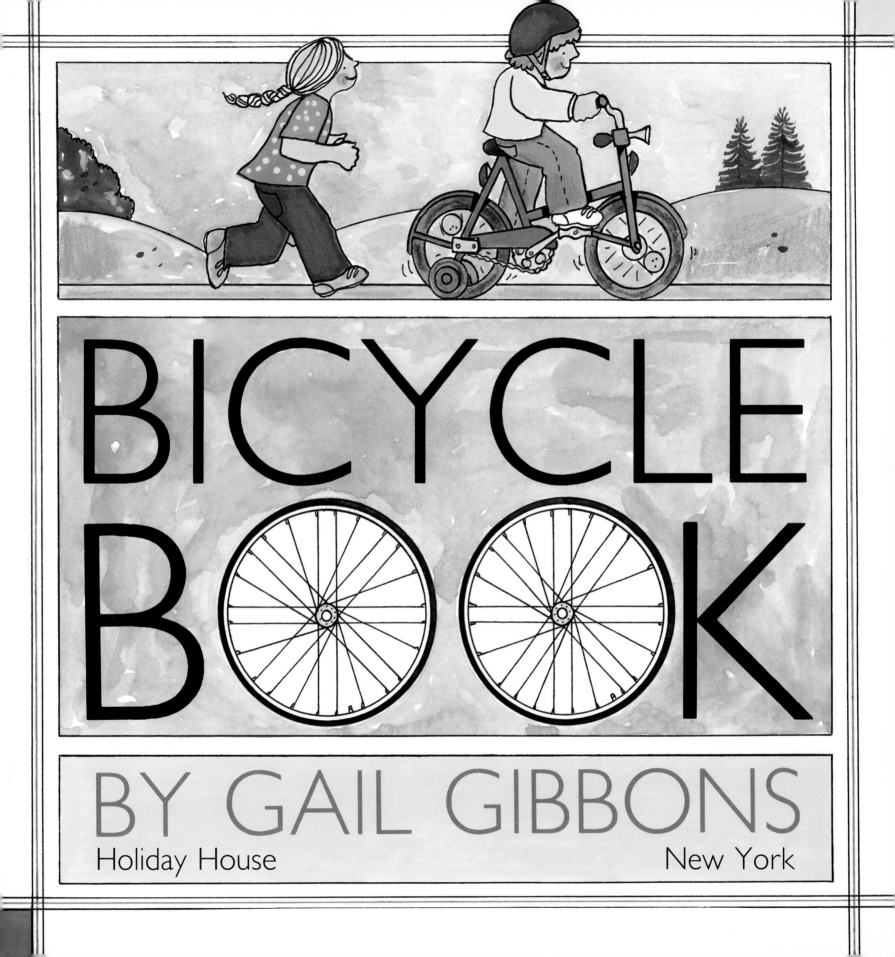

BICYCLE BOOK

BY GAIL GIBBONS

Holiday House   New York

To two bikers, Harriet and Warren Williams

Special thanks to Michael Crossman and Peter Richardson
of Onion River Sports, Barre, Vermont

Copyright © 1995 by Gail Gibbons
All rights reserved
Printed in the United States of America
First Edition

Library of Congress Cataloging-in-Publication Data
Gibbons, Gail.
Bicycle book / Gail Gibbons.—1st ed.
p.   cm.
ISBN 0-8234-1199-0 (hardcover ; permanent paper)
1. Bicycles—Juvenile literature. [1. Bicycles and bicycling.]
I. Title.
TL410.G53   1995   95-5911   CIP   AC
629.227'2—dc20

BICYCLE also called
BIKE

A bicycle is a two-wheeled vehicle that gets its power when the rider pushes the pedals around in a circle. The word bicycle means "two wheel." Bi means "two" and cycle means "wheel or circle."

The first idea for a bicycle was similar to this and is believed to have been drawn by the Italian artist and inventor, Leonardo da Vinci, about 500 years ago. His sketch looked a bit like the bicycles we see today.

WOODEN WHEEL

The first bicycle was built in France about 1800. It didn't have pedals. The rider powered the "hobbyhorse" by using his feet to push along the ground in a running motion.

CRANKS

VELOCIPEDE
IRON TIRE ON A
WOODEN WHEEL

SOLID RUBBER TIRE
ON A METAL WHEEL

HIGH-WHEELER also called
PENNY-FARTHING

About 1840 the first bicycle with pedals was built. The pedals moved the rear wheel by using cranks. Next a bicycle was invented that used pedals to power the bike by turning the front wheel. It was called the velocipede. About 1870 the high-wheeler, also called the penny-farthing, was built. It had a big front wheel that made it go faster.

SAFETY BICYCLE

CHAIN

SPROCKET WHEEL

SPROCKET WHEEL

AIR-FILLED RUBBER TIRE

Then about 1880 the first bicycle that looks like a modern bike was built. It was called the "safety bicycle." The wheels on this bike were about the same size. Pedals moved the rear wheel by means of sprocket wheels and a chain.

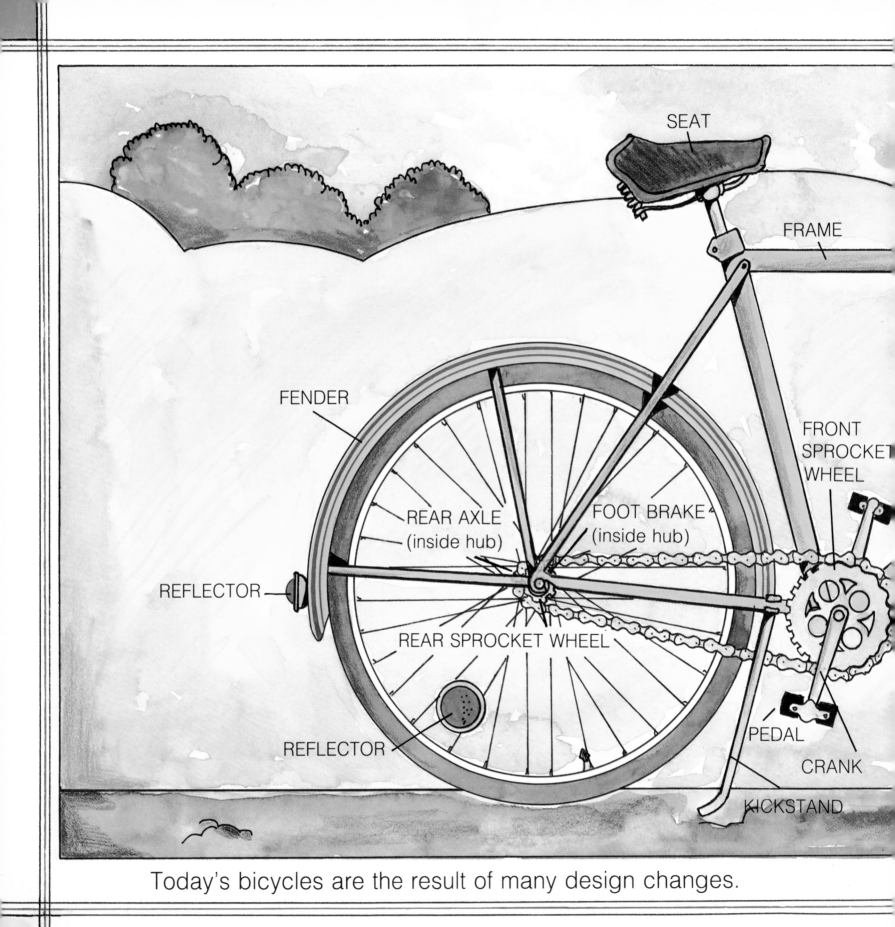

SEAT

FRAME

FENDER

FRONT SPROCKET WHEEL

REAR AXLE
(inside hub)

FOOT BRAKE
(inside hub)

REFLECTOR

REAR SPROCKET WHEEL

REFLECTOR

PEDAL

CRANK

KICKSTAND

Today's bicycles are the result of many design changes.

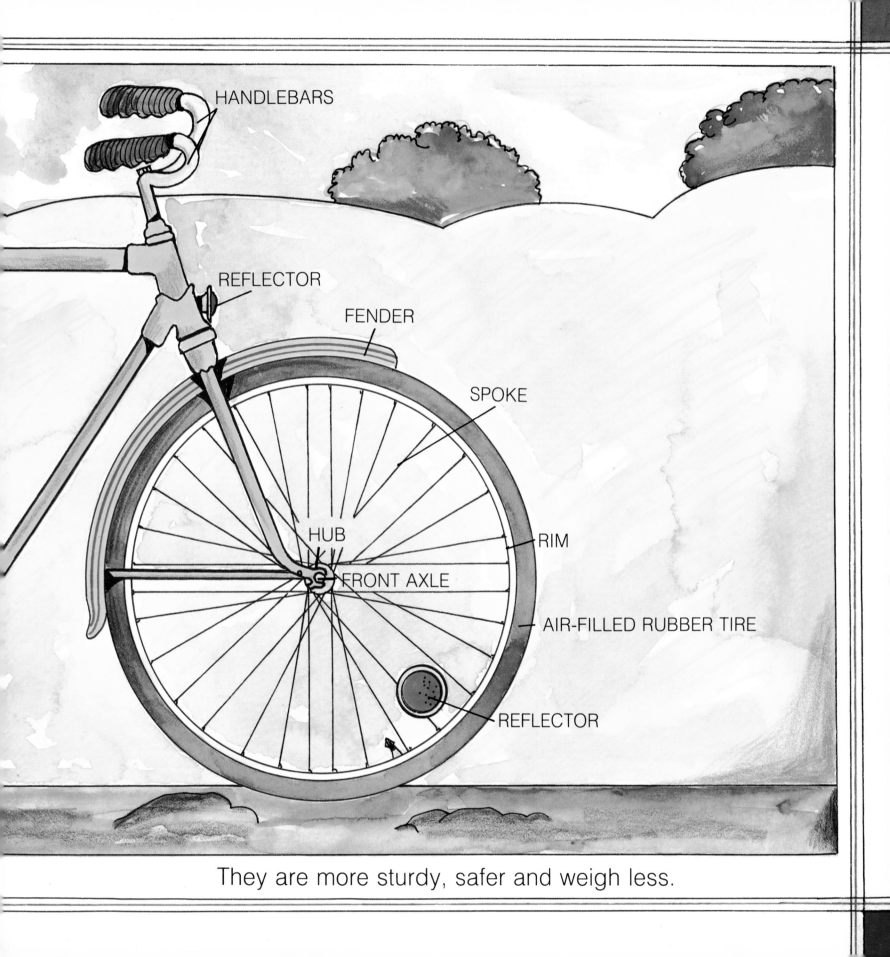

HANDLEBARS

REFLECTOR

FENDER

SPOKE

HUB

RIM

FRONT AXLE

AIR-FILLED RUBBER TIRE

REFLECTOR

They are more sturdy, safer and weigh less.

CHAIN

AXLE

SPROCKET WHEEL

PEDAL

CRANK

SPROCKET WHEEL

To give a bicycle its power, the rider pushes the pedals around and around. These pedals are attached to cranks that turn a sprocket wheel. The sprocket wheel is connected by the chain to a smaller sprocket wheel at the axle of the bicycle's rear wheel.

As the larger sprocket wheel turns, the rear sprocket wheel turns more quickly because it is smaller.

GEARSHIFT

DERAILLEUR GEAR SYSTEM
(de·RAIL·er)

CABLE

SPROCKET WHEEL

All bicycles have at least two sprocket wheels, one at the pedals and one at the rear axle. When there are more than two sprocket wheels there is a gear system. This makes pedaling easier at different times. Many bikes have a derailleur gear system that moves the chain from one sprocket wheel to another. This happens when the rider moves the cable-operated gearshift.

HANDLEBARS

GEARSHIFT

INTERNAL GEAR SYSTEM

AXLE

Some bikes have an internal gear system at the rear wheel axle. The gears are shifted by moving the gearshift or twisting the handlebars.

HAND BRAKE

CABLE

CABLE

RUBBER PAD also called
BRAKE PAD

RUBBER PAD also called
BRAKE PAD

RIM

RIM

Turning the handlebars makes the front wheel turn. To stop,
either foot brakes or hand brakes are used. The foot brake
stops a bike when one of the pedals is pushed backward.
Each hand brake is connected to brake pads by a cable.
When the hand lever is squeezed, the brake pads press
against the rim of the wheel.

ONE-SPEED BICYCLE

There are five basic kinds of bikes. First is the simple bike that has only one speed and foot brake pedals.

TOURING BICYCLE

RACING BICYCLE

A touring bike is lightweight and usually has ten or more speeds. It is used for long bike trips and for fun and pleasure. Touring bikes have thinner tires, too. A racing bike is lighter than a touring bike and may have many different speeds. It has very thin tires.

MOUNTAIN BICYCLE

DIRT BICYCLE also called
BMX BIKE

A mountain bicycle has a strong frame and wide tires. It is designed for trail riding in rough areas. A dirt bike, also called a BMX bike, has a small frame and small wheels. It has long handlebars and a high seat. Most have only one speed. They are for racing on dirt tracks and having fun.

Bicycles are used in different ways. Many are used for work.

Many are used to get to work.

Often bicycles are used for fun . . .

and sports, too.

Bike races are exciting. These bicycles are designed to go very fast.

There are road races and track races.

BICYCLE CARE CHECKLIST

CHECK THE TIRES FOR THE CORRECT AMOUNT OF AIR PRESSURE.

THE CHAIN SHOULD BE CLEAN AND OILED.

It is important to take care of a bicycle so it is safe to ride.

MAKE SURE THE BRAKES
ARE WORKING.

CHECK THE WHEELS.
THEY SHOULDN'T WOBBLE.

CHECK THE TIRES FOR CUTS
AND WEAR.

CHECK THE NUTS FOR
TIGHTNESS ON THE
WHEELS

It is good to have someone at a bicycle shop check a bike
once a year.

SAFETY RULES

1 WEAR A BICYCLE HELMET.

2 OBEY ALL SIGNS.

STOP

3 KEEP TO THE RIGHT. RIDE IN THE DIRECTION THE TRAFFIC IS GOING, NOT AGAINST IT.

4 OBEY ALL LOCAL LAWS FOR BIKERS.

5 WATCH OUT FOR POTHOLES AND OTHER PROBLEMS.

All bikers should follow safety rules.

6 DON'T OVERLOAD YOUR BIKE.

7 WATCH OUT FOR PEOPLE OPENING CAR DOORS.

8 LOOK BOTH WAYS AT CROSSROADS.

9 USE HAND SIGNALS.

RIGHT TURN

LEFT TURN

STOP OR SLOW

10 IT'S SAFEST TO RIDE DURING DAYLIGHT HOURS. IF YOU ARE CAUGHT OUT AFTER DARK, YOUR BIKE SHOULD HAVE LIGHTS AND REFLECTORS. ALWAYS TELL SOMEONE WHERE YOU ARE GOING.

Bicycling is fun, but it's important to be a safe rider.

Bicycle designs are always changing. New ideas for safer, more comfortable and faster bicycles are being tried out all the time.

Biking is fun. You can go almost anywhere under your own power.

...AND THE WHEELS GO ROUND

One early bicycle was called the boneshaker. It was very uncomfortable to ride.

The first bicycle race champion was James Moore. In 1868 he won a velocipede race in Paris, France.

The Tour de France is a very famous bicycle race. It lasts for 23 days and covers about 2200 miles all over France.

Many stunts have been done on bicycles. One rider bicycled down 1710 steps of the Eiffel Tower in Paris, France.

AND ROUND...

One of the hardest bicycle races is the Paris-Cape Town rally. The three-week race goes through the Sahara Desert.

In the United States more than 85 million people ride bicycles.

In China more than 300 million bicycles are used. Cars are too expensive.

OTHER KINDS OF BIKES

A UNICYCLE has only
one wheel.

A TANDEM BICYCLE,
a bicycle built for two
or more, has extra
seats, pedals and han-
dlebars.

A TRICYCLE has three
wheels.

An EXERCISE BICY-
CLE doesn't go any-
where. It's designed
for exercise indoors.